C000178068

Design: Jill Coote
Recipe Photography: Peter Barry
Recipe styling: Jacqueline Bellefontaine,
Helen Burdett, Bridgeen Deery and
Wendy Devenish
Jacket and Illustration Artwork: Jane Winton,
courtesy of Bernard Thornton Artists, London
Editorial: Laura Potts

CLB 3352
Published by Grange Books,
an imprint of Grange Books Limited,
The Grange, Grange Yard, London.
© 1993 CLB Publishing,
Godalming, Surrey, England.
All rights reserved.
Printed and bound in Singapore
Published 1993
ISBN 1-85627-398-9

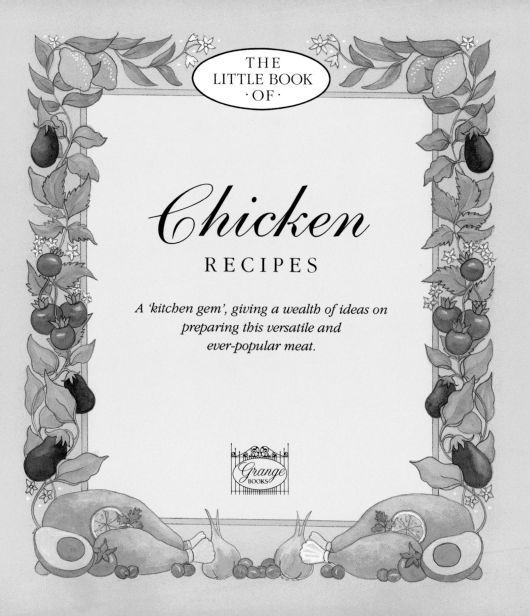

THE LITTLE BOOK ·OF·

Chicken

RECIPES

*A 'kitchen gem', giving a wealth of ideas on
preparing this versatile and
ever-popular meat.*

Grange BOOKS

Introduction

Though chicken is now one of our most popular and versatile meats, it is not so long ago that it was considered a luxury, and was reserved by many families as a special treat or as an alternative Sunday roast. Intensive methods of poultry farming, however, have changed this, making chicken both cheaper and more widely available. As a result, chicken is now one of the most frequently eaten meats, making a regular appearance on many people's everyday menus.

The popularity of chicken is due in part to its versatility. The multitude of pre-prepared cuts now available include legs, thighs, breasts, quarters and halves, and each of these can be utilised in a wide variety of ways. Some of the best-loved dishes, for example, are hearty casseroles, which make excellent use of legs and thighs by slowly simmering them with herbs or wine to give a full flavour.

Dishes that use tender breast meat, on the other hand, do not have to be time consuming and are most successful when the delicate flavour of the meat is enhanced with fresh herbs, a little onion or lemon, or a simple sauce.

The fact that chicken is low in fat and high in protein also plays a large part in its popularity. As people become aware of the health risks presented by a diet high in cholesterol, many make a conscious decision to eat less red meat and switch instead to healthier low-fat protein sources such as chicken.

The recipes in this book have been chosen for their mouthwatering variety, providing inspiration for everyday meals and great ideas for special occasions. The recipes are easy to follow and are accompanied by informative step-by-step pictures, which clarify some of the culinary techniques used.

Chicken Satay

SERVES 4

This typical Indonesian dish is very spicy.

PREPARATION: 25 mins
COOKING: 15 mins

30ml/2 tbsps soy sauce
30ml/2 tbsps sesame oil
30ml/2 tbsps lime juice
5ml/1 tsp ground cumin
5ml/1 tsp turmeric powder
10ml/2 tsps ground coriander
450g/1lb chicken breast, cut into 2.5cm/1"
    cubes
30ml/2 tbsps peanut oil
1 small onion, very finely chopped
5ml/1 tsp chilli powder
120g/4oz crunchy peanut butter
5ml/1 tsp brown sugar
Lime wedges and coriander leaves, for garnish

---

1. Put the soy sauce, sesame oil, lime juice, cumin, turmeric and coriander into a large bowl and mix well.

Step 5 Thread the marinated meat onto 4 large, or 8 small, kebab skewers.

2. Add the cubed chicken to the soy sauce marinade and stir well to coat the meat evenly.

3. Cover and allow to stand in a refrigerator for at least 1 hour, but preferably overnight.

4. Drain the meat, reserving the marinade.

5. Thread the meat onto 4 large or 8 small skewers and set aside.

6. Heat the peanut oil in a small saucepan and add the onion and chilli powder. Cook gently until the onion is slightly softened.

7. Stir the reserved marinade into the oil and onion mixture, along with the peanut butter and brown sugar. Heat gently, stirring constantly, until all the ingredients are well blended.

8. If the sauce is too thick, stir in 2-4 tbsps boiling water.

9. Arrange the skewers of meat on a grill pan and cook under a preheated moderate grill for 10-15 minutes. After the first 5 minutes of cooking, baste the meat with a little peanut sauce.

10. During the cooking time turn the meat frequently to cook it on all sides and prevent it browning.

11. Garnish with the lime and coriander leaves, and serve the remaining sauce separately.

Terrine of Spinach and Chicken

SERVES 6-8

This superb terrine makes a delicious appetizer.

PREPARATION: 25 mins
COOKING: 1 hr

225g/8oz chicken breasts, boned and skinned
2 egg whites
120g/4oz fresh white breadcrumbs
450g/1lb fresh spinach, washed
15ml/1 tbsp each of fresh finely chopped
   chervil, chives and tarragon
Freshly ground black pepper
280ml/½ pint double cream
60g/2oz finely chopped walnuts
Pinch nutmeg

---

1. Cut the chicken into small pieces.

2. Put the cut chicken, 1 egg white and half of the breadcrumbs into a food processor. Blend until well mixed.

3. Put the spinach into a large saucepan, cover with a tight-fitting lid and cook the spinach for 3 minutes, or until it has just wilted.

4. Remove the chicken mixture from the food processor and rinse the bowl.

5. Put the spinach into the food processor along with the herbs, the remaining egg white and breadcrumbs. Blend until smooth.

6. Season the chicken mixture and add half of the cream. Mix well to blend thoroughly.

Step 3 The spinach should be cooked until it is just wilted.

7. Add the walnuts, nutmeg and remaining cream to the spinach and beat well.

8. Line a 450g/1lb loaf tin with greaseproof paper. Lightly oil this with a little vegetable oil.

9. Pour the chicken mixture into the base of the tin and spread evenly. Carefully pour the spinach mixture over the chicken mixture, and smooth the top.

10. Cover the tin with lightly oiled aluminium foil and seal this tightly around the edges.

11. Stand the tin in a dish and pour enough warm water into the dish to come halfway up the sides. Cook at 160°C/325°F/Gas Mark 3 for 1 hour, or until firm.

12. Put the terrine into the refrigerator and chill for at least 12 hours.

13. Carefully lift the terrine out of the tin and peel off the paper.

Crumb Fried Chicken

SERVES 6

A tasty dish from Southern Germany.

PREPARATION: 30 mins
COOKING: 40 mins

1.5kg/3lb chicken
2 eggs, mixed with a pinch of salt
120g/4oz breadcrumbs
60g/2oz Parmesan cheese
1.25ml/¼ tsp powdered ginger
60g/4 tbsps butter or margarine
45ml/3 tbsps oil
Lemon and parsley for garnish

---

1. Preheat the oven to 200°C/400°F/Gas Mark 6. To joint the chicken, first cut off the legs, bending them backwards to break the joint. Cut in between the joint to completely remove the legs.

2. Cut down the breastbone with sharp poultry shears to separate the two halves. Use the poultry shears to cut through the rib cage. Use

Step 1 Bend the leg backwards to break the ball and socket joint and cut in between.

Step 2 Use the notch to cut through the wing joint.

the notch in the shears to separate the wing joints from the back.

3. Cut the quarters into two pieces each. Use a sharp knife to separate the drumstick from the thigh. Cut the breasts in half, leaving some of the white meat attached to the wing joint. Cut through the bones with poultry shears.

4. Mix the breadcrumbs, Parmesan cheese and powdered ginger together. First dip the chicken into the egg and then coat with the crumbs.

5. Heat the oil in a large frying pan and add the butter. When hot, place in the chicken, skin side down first. Cook both sides until golden brown.

6. Transfer with a slotted spoon to a baking sheet and place in the oven for 20-30 minutes, or until the juices run clear when tested with a knife. Serve garnished with small bunches of parsley and lemon wedges or slices.

Saffron Chicken

SERVES 4

Saffron gives rice and sauces a lovely golden colour and delicate taste.

PREPARATION: 20-25 mins
COOKING: 25-35 mins

30ml/2 tbsps oil
900g-1.5kg/2-3lb chicken, cut into 8 pieces and
    skinned if desired
1 small onion, finely chopped
10ml/2 tsps paprika
1 clove garlic, crushed
8 tomatoes, peeled, seeded and chopped
300g/10oz rice
700ml/1¼ pints boiling water
Large pinch saffron or 1.25ml/¼ tsp ground
    saffron
180g/6oz frozen peas
30ml/2 tbsps chopped parsley

1. Heat the oil in a large frying pan. Season the chicken and place it in the hot oil, skin side down first. Cook over moderate heat, turning the chicken frequently to brown it lightly. Set the chicken aside.

2. Add the onions to the oil and cook slowly until softened but not coloured.

3. Add the paprika and cook for about 2

Step 4 When the garlic and tomatoes are added, cook over a high heat to evaporate the liquid.

minutes, stirring frequently until the paprika loses some of its red colour. Add the garlic and the tomatoes.

4. Cook the mixture over high heat for about 5 minutes to evaporate the liquid from the tomatoes. The mixture should be of dropping consistency when done. Add the rice, water and saffron and stir together.

5. Return the chicken to the casserole and bring to the boil over high heat. Reduce to simmering, cover tightly and cook for about 20 minutes. Remove chicken and add the peas and parsley. Cook a further 5-10 minutes, or until rice is tender. Combine with the chicken to serve.

Chicken Cacciatore

SERVES 4-6

A rich Italian dish with mushrooms and olives.

PREPARATION: 30 mins
COOKING: 1hr 15 mins

45ml/3 tbsps oil
120g/4oz mushrooms, quartered, if large
1.5kg/3lb chicken pieces
1 onion
2 cloves garlic
140ml/¼ pint vermouth
15ml/1 tbsp white wine vinegar
140ml/¼ pint chicken stock
5ml/1 tsp oregano
1 sprig fresh rosemary
450g/1lb tinned tomatoes
60g/2oz black olives, pitted
30g/2 tbsps chopped parsley

1. Heat the oil in a heavy-based frying pan and cook the mushrooms for about 1-2 minutes. Remove them and set aside.

2. Brown the chicken in the oil and transfer the browned pieces to an ovenproof casserole.

3. Chop the onion and garlic finely. Pour off all but 15ml/1 tbsp of the oil in the frying pan and reheat the pan. Cook the onion and garlic until softened but not coloured.

4. Add the vermouth and vinegar and boil to reduce by half.

5. Add the chicken stock, tomatoes, oregano, rosemary and season. Break up the tomatoes and bring the sauce to the boil. Allow to cook for 2 minutes.

6. Pour the sauce over the chicken in the casserole, cover and cook at 180°C/350°F/Gas Mark 4 for about 1 hour.

7. To remove the stones from the olives, roll them on a flat surface to loosen the stones and then use a swivel vegetable peeler to extract them. Alternatively use a cherry pitter.

8. Add mushrooms and olives during the last 5 minutes of cooking.

9. Remove the rosemary before serving and sprinkle with chopped parsley.

Step 3 Cut onion in half lengthways leaving root end intact. Cut in thin horizontal slices. Then cut in lengthwise strips.

Chicken Cobbler

SERVES 6

A warming winter dish with a creamy sauce and light topping.

Preparation: 25 mins
Cooking: 1 hr

4 chicken joints, 2 breasts and 2 legs
1.5 litres/2½ pints water
1 bay leaf
4 whole peppercorns
2 carrots, peeled and diced
24 button onions, peeled
90g/6 tbsps frozen sweetcorn
140ml/¼ pint double cream

Topping
400g/14oz plain flour
25ml/1½ tbsps baking powder
Pinch salt
75g/5 tbsps butter or margarine
340ml/12 fl oz milk
1 egg, beaten with a pinch of salt

1. Place the chicken in a deep saucepan with water, bay leaf and peppercorns. Cover and bring to the boil. Reduce the heat and allow to simmer for 20-30 minutes, or until the chicken is tender. Remove the chicken from the pot and allow to cool. Skim and discard the fat from the surface of the stock. Skin the chicken and remove the meat from the bones.

Step 5 Roll out the mixture on a floured surface, cut into rounds and place on top of the chicken mixture.

2. Continue to simmer the stock until reduced by about half. Strain, then add the carrots and onions. Cook until tender and add the sweetcorn. Stir in the cream and season. Add the chicken. Pour into a casserole.

3. To prepare the topping, sift the dry ingredients into a bowl.

4. Rub in the butter or margarine until the mixture resembles small peas. Stir in enough of the milk to bind the mixture.

5. Turn out onto a floured surface and knead lightly. Roll out with a floured rolling pin and cut with a pastry cutter. Brush the surface of each round with the egg mixture. Place on top of the chicken mixture and bake for 10-15 minutes in a pre-heated over at 190°C/375°F/ Gas Mark 5. Serve immediately.

Country Captain Chicken

SERVES 6

This dish was named after a sea captain with a taste for the spicy cuisine of India.

PREPARATION: 30 mins
COOKING: 50 mins

1.5kg/3lbs chicken pieces
Seasoned flour
90ml/6 tbsps oil
1 medium onion, chopped
1 medium green pepper, seeded and chopped
1 clove garlic, crushed
10ml/2 tsps curry powder
2 × 400g/14oz tinned tomatoes
10ml/2 tsps chopped parsley
5ml/1 tsp chopped marjoram
60ml/4 tbsps currants or raisins
120g/4oz blanched almond halves

1. Remove skin from the chicken and dredge with flour, shaking off the excess.

Step 4 Add the curry powder to the vegetables in the frying pan and cook for two minutes over low heat stirring frequently.

Step 5 Toast the almonds on a baking sheet in the oven until light golden brown.

2. Heat the oil and brown the chicken on all sides until golden. Remove to an ovenproof casserole.

3. Pour off all but 30ml/2 tbsps of the oil. Add the onion, pepper and garlic and cook slowly to soften.

4. Add the curry powder and season. Cook, stirring frequently, for 2 minutes. Add the tomatoes, parsley and marjoram and bring to the boil. Pour the sauce over the chicken, cover and cook in a pre-heated 180°C/350°F/Gas Mark 4 oven for 45 minutes. Add the currants or raisins during the last 15 minutes.

5. Meanwhile, toast the almonds in the oven on a baking sheet along with the chicken. Stir them frequently and watch carefully. Sprinkle over the chicken just before serving.

Chicken with Olives

SERVES 4-6

This is a chicken sauté dish for olive lovers. Use more or less of them as your own taste dictates.

PREPARATION: 25 mins
COOKING: 50-55 mins

1.5kg/3lb chicken pieces
30ml/2 tbsps olive oil
30g/2 tbsps butter or margarine
1 clove garlic, crushed
140ml/¼ pint white wine
140ml/¼ pint chicken stock
30ml/2 tbsps chopped parsley
20 pitted black and green olives
4 courgettes, cut in 1.25cm/½ inch pieces

Step 1 Cook the chicken, skin side down first, until golden brown.

To peel a garlic clove easily, first crush it gently with the side of a large knife. The peel will split, making it easier to remove.

1. Heat the oil in a large frying pan and add the butter or margarine. When foaming, add the chicken skin side down. Brown one side of the chicken and turn over to brown the other side. Cook the chicken in two batches if necessary.

2. Turn the chicken skin side up and add the garlic, wine and stock, season, then bring to the boil. Cover the pan and allow to simmer over gentle heat for about 30-35 minutes.

3. Add the courgettes and cook 10 minutes. Once the chicken and courgettes are done, add the olives and cook to heat through. Add the parsley and remove to a dish to serve.

Chicken with Aubergine and Ham Stuffing

SERVES 4-6

Aubergines and ham make an unusual stuffing and add interest to roast chicken.

PREPARATION: 30 mins
COOKING: 5-6 mins for the stuffing and about
    1 hr for the chicken

1.5kg/3lb roasting chicken
1 small aubergine
60g/4 tbsps butter
1 small onion, finely chopped
120g/4oz ham, chopped
120g/4oz fresh breadcrumbs
10ml/2 tsps chopped mixed herbs
1-2 eggs, beaten

1. Cut the aubergine in half lengthways and remove stem. Lightly score the surface with a sharp knife and sprinkle with salt. Leave to stand for about 30 minutes for the salt to draw out any bitter juices.

2. Melt half the butter in a saucepan and cook the onion slowly to soften slightly.

Step 1 Sprinkle the cut surface of the aubergine lightly with salt and leave to stand.

Step 4 Remove the fat from just inside the cavity opening.

3. Rinse the aubergine and pat dry. Cut into 1.25cm/½ inch cubes. Cook with the onion until fairly soft. Add the remaining stuffing ingredients, beating in the egg gradually until the mixture just holds together. Season to taste.

4. Remove the fat from just inside the chicken cavity. Fill the neck end with the stuffing. Place any extra in a greased casserole. Tuck the wing tips under the chicken to hold the neck flap down. Tie the legs together and place the chicken in a roasting pan.

5. Spread over the remaining softened butter and roast in a pre-heated 180°C/350°F/Gas Mark 4 oven for about 1 hour, or until the juices from the chicken run clear when the thickest part of the thigh is pierced with a sharp knife. Cook extra stuffing, covered for the last 35 minutes of cooking time. Leave the chicken to stand for 10 minutes before carving. If desired, make a gravy with the pan juices.

Spicy Spanish Chicken

SERVES 6

Chilli peppers, coriander and tomatoes add a Spanish flavour to grilled chicken.

PREPARATION: 1 hr
COOKING: 14-20 mins

6 boned chicken breasts
Grated rind and juice of 1 lime
30ml/2 tbsps olive oil
90ml/6 tbsps whole grain mustard
10ml/2 tsps paprika
4 ripe tomatoes, peeled, seeded and quartered
2 shallots, chopped
1 clove garlic, crushed
½ chilli pepper, seeded and chopped
5ml/1 tsp wine vinegar
30ml/2 tbsps chopped fresh coriander
Whole coriander leaves to garnish

1. Place chicken breasts in a shallow dish with the lime rind and juice, oil, mustard, paprika and coarsely ground black pepper. Marinate for

Step 2
Tomatoes peel easily when placed first in boiling water and then in cold.

Step 4 Grill skin side of chicken until brown and crisp before turning pieces over.

about 1 hour, turning occasionally.

2. To peel tomatoes easily, drop them into boiling water for about 5 seconds or less depending on ripeness. Place immediately in cold water. Skins should come off easily.

3. Coarsely chop tomatoes, shallots, garlic, chilli pepper, then add the vinegar and salt. Stir in the coriander.

4. Place chicken on a grill pan and reserve the marinade. Cook chicken skin side uppermost for about 7-10 minutes, depending on how close the chicken is to the heat source. Baste frequently with the remaining marinade. Grill other side in the same way. Sprinkle with salt after grilling.

5. Place chicken on serving plates and garnish top with coriander leaves. Serve with a spoonful of the tomato relish on one side.

Lime Roasted Chicken

SERVES 4

Its simple, tangy flavour make this an ideal summer dish.

PREPARATION: 25 mins, plus 4 hrs to marinate
COOKING: 40 mins

---

4 chicken breast portions
4 limes
10ml/2 tsps white wine vinegar
75ml/5 tbsps olive oil
10ml/2 tsp fresh chopped basil

---

1. Rub the chicken portions all over with salt and black pepper. Place in a shallow ovenproof dish, and set aside.

2. Carefully pare away thin strips of the rind only from 2 of the limes, using a lemon parrer. Cut these 2 limes in half and squeeze the juice.

3. Add the lime juice to the vinegar and 4 tbsps of the olive oil in a small dish, along with the strips of rind, and mix well.

4. Pour the oil and lime juice mixture over the

Step 5 After marinating for 4 hours, the chicken will look slightly cooked and the meat will have turned a pale opaque colour.

Step 7 Fry the lime slices very quickly in the hot oil until they just begin to soften.

chicken. Cover and refrigerate for about 4 hours or overnight.

5. Remove the covering from the dish in which the chicken is marinating, and baste the chicken well with the marinade mixture. Place into a preheated oven 190°C/375°F/Gas Mark 5 and cook for 30-35 minutes, or until the chicken is well roasted and tender.

6. In the meantime, peel away the rind and white pith from the remaining 2 limes. Cut the limes into thin slices using a sharp knife.

7. Heat the remaining oil in a small frying pan and add the lime slices and basil. Cook quickly for 1 minute, or until the fragrance rises up from the basil and the limes just begin to soften.

8. Serve the chicken portions on a serving platter, garnished with the fried lime slices and a little fresh basil.

Chicken and Pepper Salad

SERVES 6

This piquant lunch or light supper dish can be prepared in advance.

PREPARATION: 30 mins

450g/1lb cooked chicken, cut in strips
140ml/¼ pint mayonnaise
140ml/¼ pint natural yogurt
5ml/1 tsp chilli powder
5ml/1 tsp paprika
Pinch cayenne pepper
2.5ml/½ tsp tomato purée
5ml/1 tsp onion purée
1 green pepper, seeded and finely sliced
1 red pepper, seeded and finely sliced
180g/6oz frozen sweetcorn, defrosted
180g/6oz long grain rice, cooked

Step 4 Arrange rice on a serving plate and spoon salad into the centre.

Step 2 Fold all ingredients together gently so that they do not break up. Use a large spoon or rubber spatula.

1. Place the chicken strips in a large salad bowl.

2. Mix the mayonnaise, yogurt, spices, tomato and onion purées together and leave to stand briefly for flavours to blend. Fold dressing into the chicken.

3. Add the peppers and sweetcorn and mix gently until all the ingredients are coated with dressing.

4. Place the rice on a serving dish and pile the salad into the centre. Serve immediately.

Chicken and Avocado Salad

SERVES 4

The creamy herb dressing complements this easy summer salad.

PREPARATION: 30 mins

8 anchovy fillets, soaked in milk, rinsed and
    dried
1 spring onion, chopped
30g/2 tbsps chopped fresh tarragon
45g/3 tbsps chopped chives
60g/4 tbsps chopped parsley
280ml/½ pint mayonnaise
140ml/¼ pint natural yogurt
30ml/2 tbsps tarragon vinegar
Pinch sugar and cayenne pepper
1 large head lettuce
450g/1lb cooked chicken
1 avocado, peeled and cubed
15ml/1 tbsp lemon juice

Step 3 Arrange lettuce on individual plates and top with shredded chicken.

Step 1 The dressing should be very well blended after working in a food processor. Alternatively, use a hand blender.

1. Combine all the ingredients, except the lettuce, avocado and chicken in a food processor. Work the ingredients until smooth, and well mixed. Leave in the refrigerator at least 1 hour for the flavours to blend.

2. Shred the lettuce or tear into bite-size pieces and arrange on plates.

3. Top the lettuce with the cooked chicken cut into strips or cubes.

4. Spoon the dressing over the chicken. Toss the avocado cubes with lemon juice and garnish the salad. Serve any remaining dressing separately.

Tarragon Chicken Pancakes

SERVES 4

These easy-to-make pancakes are sophisticated enough for a dinner party.

PREPARATION: 25 mins
COOKING: 25 mins

Pancake batter
120g/4oz plain wholemeal flour
1 egg
280ml/½ pint milk
Oil, for frying

Filling
45g/1½oz plain flour
280ml/½ pint skimmed milk
225g/8oz cooked chicken, chopped
1 avocado pear, peeled, halved, stoned and
   chopped
10ml/2 tsps lemon juice
15ml/1 tbsp chopped fresh tarragon

1. Put the wholemeal flour into a large bowl, and make a slight well in the centre. Break the egg into the well and begin to beat it carefully into the flour, incorporating only a little flour at a time.

2. Add the milk gradually to the egg and flour mixture, beating well between additions, until all the milk is incorporated and the batter is smooth.

3. Heat a little oil in a small frying pan, or crêpe pan, and cook about 2 tbsps of the batter at a time, tipping and rotating the pan, so that

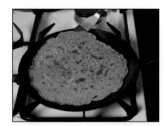

Step 3 Using a small frying pan, or crêpe pan, heat a little oil and fry 2 tbsps of the batter at a time.

the batter spreads evenly over the base to form a pancake. Flip the pancake over, to cook the second side.

4. Repeat this process until all the batter has been used up. Keep the pancakes warm, until required.

5. Blend the plain flour with a little of the milk, then gradually add the rest.

6. Pour the flour and milk mixture into a small pan, and cook over a moderate heat, stirring continuously, until the sauce has thickened. Season to taste.

7. Stir the chopped chicken, avocado, lemon juice and tarragon into the sauce.

8. Fold each pancake in half, and then in half again, to form a triangle.

9. Carefully open part of the triangle out to form an envelope, and fill this with the chicken and avocado mixture.

Aubergine and Chicken Chilli

SERVES 4

This unusual stir-fry dish is both delicious and filling.

PREPARATION: 10 mins
COOKING: 15 mins

---

2 medium-sized aubergines
60ml/4 tbsps sesame oil
2 cloves garlic, peeled and crushed
4 spring onions
1 green chilli pepper, finely chopped
350g/12oz boned and skinned chicken breast
60ml/4 tbsps light soy sauce
30ml/2 tbsps stock, or water
15ml/1 tbsp tomato purée
5ml/1 tsp cornflour
5ml/1 tsp sugar

---

1. Cut the aubergine into quarters lengthways, using a sharp knife. Slice the aubergine quarters into pieces approximately 1.25cm/½ -inch thick.

2. Put the aubergine slices into a bowl and sprinkle liberally with salt. Stir well to coat evenly. Cover with cling film and leave to stand for 30 minutes.

3. Rinse the aubergine slices very thoroughly under running water, then pat dry with a clean tea cloth.

4. Heat half of the oil in a wok, or large frying pan, and gently cook the garlic until it is soft, but not coloured.

Step 6 Cut the spring onions diagonally into small pieces, approximately 1.25cm/½ inch long.

5. Add the aubergine slices to the wok and cook, stirring frequently, for 3-4 minutes.

6. Slice the spring onions into thin diagonal strips and stir into the cooked aubergine together with the chilli, and cook for 1 minute. Remove the aubergine and onion and set aside, keeping warm.

7. Cut the chicken breast into thin slices with a sharp knife.

8. Heat the remaining oil in the wok, and fry the chicken pieces for approximately 2 minutes or until they have turned white and are cooked.

9. Return the aubergine and onions to the pan and cook, stirring continuously, for 2 minutes or until heated through completely.

10. Mix together the remaining ingredients and pour these over the chicken and aubergines in the wok, stirring constantly until the sauce has thickened and cleared. Serve immediately.

Chicken Liver Stir-Fry

SERVES 4

Chicken livers need quick cooking, so they are a perfect choice for the Chinese stir-frying method.

PREPARATION: 25 mins
COOKING: 4-5 mins

225g/8oz chicken livers
45ml/3 tbsps oil
60g/2oz split blanched almonds
1 clove garlic, peeled
60g/2oz mangetout
8-10 Chinese leaves
10g/2 tsps cornflour
30ml/2 tbsps soy sauce
140ml/¼ pint chicken stock

1. Pick over the chicken livers and remove any discoloured areas or bits of fat. Cut the chicken livers into even-sized pieces.

2. Heat a wok and pour in the oil. When the oil

Step 1 Cut off any yellowish or greenish portions from the livers and divide them into even-sized pieces.

Step 3 Quickly stir-fry the livers until lightly browned on the outside. May be served slightly pink in the middle.

is hot, turn the heat down and add the almonds. Cook, stirring continuously, over gentle heat until the almonds are a nice golden brown. Remove and drain on paper towels.

3. Add the garlic, cook for 1-2 minutes to flavour the oil and remove. Add the chicken livers and cook for about 2-3 minutes, stirring frequently. Remove the chicken livers and set them aside. Add the mangetout to the wok and stir-fry for 1 minute. Shred the Chinese leaves finely, add to the wok and cook for 1 minute. Remove the vegetables and set them aside.

4. Mix the cornflour with a little water and the soy sauce and stock. Pour into the wok and bring to the boil. Cook unil thickened and clear. Return all the other ingredients to the sauce and reheat for 30 seconds. Serve immediately.

Poussins with Devilled Sauce

SERVES 4

Although this recipe takes quite a while to prepare, the end result will make your effort worthwhile.

PREPARATION: 25 mins, plus 1 hr standing time
COOKING: 60-70 mins.

---

4 poussins
5ml/1 tsp each of paprika, mustard powder and ground ginger
2.5ml/½ tsp ground turmeric
1.25ml/¼ tsp ground allspice
60g/4 tbsps unsalted butter
30ml/2 tbsps chilli sauce
15ml/1 tbsp plum chutney
15ml/1 tbsp brown sauce
15ml/1 tbsp Worcestershire sauce
15ml/1 tbsp soy sauce
Dash Tabasco sauce
45ml/3 tbsps chicken stock

---

1. Tie the legs of each poussin together and tuck them under the wing tips.

2. Put the paprika, mustard powder, ginger, turmeric and allspice, into a small bowl and mix together well.

3. Rub the spice mixture evenly on all sides of the four poussins, taking great care to push some behind the wings and into the joints.

4. Refrigerate the poussins for at least 1 hour.

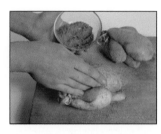

Step 3 Rub the poussins all over with the spice mixture, pressing it down into the wings and joints.

5. Arrange the poussins in a roasting pan. Melt the butter and brush it evenly over the birds. Roast in a preheated oven, 180°C/350°F/Gas Mark 4, for 20 minutes, brushing with the roasting juices during this time.

6. In a small bowl, mix together the chilli sauce, plum chutney, brown sauce, Worcestershire sauce, soy sauce, Tabasco and chicken stock.

7. Brush about half of this sauce over the poussins. Return to the oven and cook for a further 40 minutes.

8. Brush the poussins twice more with the remaining sauce mixture during this final cooking time so that the skins become brown and crisp.

Chicken with Cloud Ears

SERVES 6

Cloud ears is the delightful name for an edible tree fungus which is mushroom-like in taste and texture.

PREPARATION: 25 mins
COOKING: 5 mins

---

12 cloud ears, wood ears or other dried Chinese
    mushrooms, soaked in boiling water for 5
    minutes
450g/1lb boned chicken breasts, thinly sliced
1 egg white
10ml/2 tsps cornflour
10ml/2 tsps white wine
10ml/2 tsps sesame oil
2.5cm/1″ piece fresh ginger, left whole
1 clove garlic, left whole
280ml/½ pint oil
280ml/½ pint chicken stock
15g/1 tbsp cornflour
45ml/3 tbsps light soy sauce

---

1. Soak the mushrooms until they soften and swell. Remove the skin from the chicken and cut it into thin slices. Mix the chicken with egg white, cornflour, wine and sesame oil.

2. Heat the wok for a few minutes and pour in the oil. Add the whole piece of ginger and whole garlic clove to the oil and cook for about 1 minute. Take them out and reduce the heat.

3. Add about a quarter of the chicken at a time and stir-fry for about 1 minute. Remove and continue cooking until all the chicken is fried. Remove all but about 30ml/2 tbsps of the oil from the wok.

4. Drain the mushrooms and squeeze them to extract all the liquid. If using mushrooms with stems, remove the stems before slicing thinly. Cut cloud ears or wood ears into smaller pieces. Add to the wok and cook for about 1 minute. Add the stock and allow it to come almost to the boil. Mix together the cornflour and soy sauce and add a spoonful of the hot stock. Add the mixture to the wok, stirring constantly, and bring to the boil. Allow to boil 1-2 minutes or until thickened and become clear.

5. Return the chicken to the wok and season. Stir thoroughly for about 1 minute and serve immediately.

Step 1 Soak mushrooms in boiling water for five minutes.

Index

Lime Roasted Chicken, a tangy, low-calorie dish